MILITARY MACHINES

AMPHIBIOUS VEHICLES

BY RYAN NAGELHOUT

Gareth Stevens
PUBLISHING

HOT TOPICS

Please visit our website, www.garethstevens.com. For a free color catalog of all our high-quality books, call toll free 1-800-542-2595 or fax 1-877-542-2596.

Nagelhout, Ryan.
Amphibious vehicles / by Ryan Nagelhout.
p. cm. — (Mighty military machines)
Includes index.
ISBN 978-1-4824-2114-9 (pbk.)
ISBN 978-1-4824-2113-2 (6-pack)
ISBN 978-1-4824-2115-6 (library binding)
1. Motor vehicles, Amphibious — Juvenile literature. 2. Vehicles, Military — Juvenile literature. I. Nagelhout, Ryan. II. Title.
UG446.5 N34 2015
623.7—d23

First Edition

Published in 2015 by
Gareth Stevens Publishing
111 East 14th Street, Suite 349
New York, NY 10003

Designer: Nicholas Domiano
Editor: Ryan Nagelhout

Photo credits: Cover background Ensuper/Shutterstock.com; series logo Makhnach_S/ Shutterstock.com; cover, pp. 1, 25, 29 Stockrek Images/Getty Images; p. 4 tristan tan/ Shutterstock.com; p. 5 Frank Scherschel/The LIFE Picture Collection/Getty Images; p. 6 JUNG YEON-JE/AFP/Getty Images; p. 7 ID1974/Shutterstock.com; p. 9 Unus Multorum/Wikimedia Commons; p. 10 Metilsteiner/Wikimedia Commons; p. 11 U.S. Navy/APphotos.com; p. 13 BotMultiChilt/Wikimedia Commons; p. 14 UniversalImagesGroup/Universal Images Group/Getty Images; p. 15 Acme/ APphotos.com; p. 17 Malcolm W. Brown/Associated Press/APphotos.com; p. 19 Sonaz/ Wikimedia Commons; p. 21 Lance Cpl. Jody Lee Smith/Wikimedia Commons; p. 23 Lance Cpl. Cesar Contreras/Wikimedia Commons; p. 26 U.S. Marines/APphotos.com; p. 27 Scott J. Ferrell/CQ-Roll Call Group/Getty Images.

Printed in the United States of America

CPSIA compliance information: Batch # CW15GS: For further information contact Gareth Stevens, New York, New York at 1-800-542-2595.

CONTENTS

LAND AND SEA

Have you ever seen a boat drive on land? What about a car that goes for a swim? It may sound crazy, but it's not! An amphibious **vehicle** works on both land and in water. It's basically a boat you can drive on land!

Amphibians are animals that live both in water and on land, like frogs and newts.

There are many kinds of amphibious vehicles. Some are made to look like boats with wheels. Others look like tanks. The US military uses amphibious vehicles to move people or things through water and onto land.

INTEL REPORT

There are even amphibious bicycles that
float on water and can ride on land!

ORUKTER AMPHIBOLOS

In 1805, Oliver Evans made one of the first amphibious vehicles. Used in Philadelphia, Pennsylvania, Evans called it *Orukter Amphibolos*, Greek for "amphibious digger." The machine was steam powered and was supposed to dig up the bottom of rivers.

OLIVER EVANS

Orukter Amphibolos never really worked very well as a digger. Some historians say it was America's first steamboat, **locomotive**, and car!

THE ALLIGATOR

In the late 1800s, Canadian loggers needed a machine that could move logs through water as well as over land. Joseph Jackson invented the "Alligator," a steam-powered boat with wooden wheels on the side. Alligators could pull themselves across land.

ALLIGATOR BOAT

INTEL REPORT

The West & Peachey Company made 230 Alligators between 1889 and 1932.

ON SCREWS

Russian inventor Alexey Burdin created a vehicle that sits on giant **screws**. The screws spin and keep the vehicle moving forward. Though it moved slowly, it could travel over mud and even open water.

INTEL REPORT

The problem with vehicles that sit on screws is that they tear up the ground as they move. They also move very slowly.

DUKW

Amphibious vehicles used in the military have **armor**. One early American vehicle was called the DUKW, or "Duck." Made in 1942, it was used in World War II to move troops and supplies onto land.

DUKWs had six wheels and were
made by General Motors.

M113

The M113 armored **personnel** carrier has been used by the US military since the 1960s. The first model entered service in 1961. The M113 was often used during the Vietnam War, where it easily moved through plant growth in the jungle.

The newest version of the M113, the A3, was first used in 1986. There are many kinds that can do special jobs, such as fix and help find other vehicles. Some M113A3s can even be used as **ambulances**.

INTEL REPORT

Many different countries have M113s, including Israel, Belgium, and Italy.

AAVs

Amphibious **Assault** Vehicles, or AAVs, were made for the US Marines in 1972. The vehicles were **designed** to enter the water from a ship and drive to shore and go on land. The marines call AAVs "amtracks," which is short for "amphibious tractor."

INTEL REPORT

AAVs have been modified, or changed, many times over the last four decades.

AAV-7

Today the marines use an AAV called the AAV-7. It's the first vehicle to reach land during beach assaults. It can carry 21 marines and has a crew of 3. The AAV-7 can move 10,000 pounds (4,540 kg) of **cargo**.

The AAV can travel up to 45 miles (72 km) per hour and 8 to 10 knots (9 to 12 miles per hour) in water. The hull, or body, is made of **aluminum**, which keeps troops safe. It can carry many different **weapons**, including smoke grenades, and can fire when on land and water.

THE FUTURE

The Expeditionary Fighting Vehicle (EFV) was designed by the US military to replace the AAV, which is more than 40 years old. The EFV program started in 1997 and was supposed to build an advanced amphibious vehicle that was safer than the AAV.

Early EFVs broke down after
only a few hours of use.

In 2011, the Marine Corps stopped making the EFV because the project cost too much and it didn't work as well as the AAV. The US military is currently working on the Amphibious Combat Vehicle, or ACV, to one day replace the AAV.

INTEL REPORT

The Defense Advanced Research Projects Agency (DARPA) wants people to design the next amphibious armored troop carrier. They even have a $4 million prize for the winner!

INSIDE AN AMPHIBIOUS VEHICLE

CARGO
BAY

GUNS

HULL

TREADS

FOR MORE INFORMATION

Books

Alpert, Barbara. *Military Amphibious Vehicles*. North Mankato, MN: Capstone Press, 2012.

Funk, Joe. *An Inside Look at the U.S. Navy SEALs*. New York, NY: Scholastic, 2011.

Shank, Carol. *U.S. Military Assault Vehicles*. North Mankato, MN: Capstone, 2013.

Websites

AAV-7

marines.com/operating-forces/equipment/vehicles/aav-7
Find out more information about the AAV-7.

DUKW

http://www.transchool.lee.army.mil/museum/transportation%20 museum/dukw.htm
Learn more about the history of DUKW vehicles at the US Army Transportation Museum.

GLOSSARY

aluminum: a type of lightweight metal

ambulance: a vehicle that moves injured or sick people

armor: a thick covering used to keep someone safe from harm

assault: a sudden attack

cargo: supplies or tools being moved

design: to create the pattern or shape of something

locomotive: an engine that moves under its own power, usually to pull train cars

personnel: a group of people working together

screw: a solid tube with a winding thread going around it

vehicle: an object that moves people from one place to another

weapon: something used to fight an enemy

INDEX